Electric Utility Rate Reform

American Enterprise Institute for Public Policy Research
Washington, D.C.

ISBN 0-8447-0193-9
Legislative Analysis No. 11, 95th Congress
20 September 1977

Price $2.00 per copy

CONTENTS

DEFINITIONS

automatic adjustment clause: a clause in a rate schedule that provides for an adjustment in the customer's bill for variations in the cost of the item from a specified base level of cost.

capacity: the load which the utility system is capable of serving; or the load for which an individual component (generator, transmission circuit, or transformer) is rated.

certificate: an order of an appropriate regulatory authority required to construct or extend facilities or to provide service.

cogeneration: the production of electric energy and other forms of energy (such as steam) by the same process.

demand: the rate at which electric energy is delivered, usually expressed in kilowatts.

energy: that which does or is capable of doing work, usually expressed in kilowatt-hours.

franchise: the right or privilege of providing service in a specified territory.

interconnection: a tie permitting the flow of energy between the facilities of two electric systems.

load factor: average demand over a period of time divided by peak demand for a utility system or a specific consumer or class of consumers.

load management technique: a method, other than a rate form or level, to reduce maximum demand on a utility or to reduce the demand of a consumer.

master metering: the use of a single meter to measure service to a building with multiple users.

pancaking a rate increase: filing increased rates before a determination of the lawfulness of previously filed increased rates.

power pool: two or more electric systems which are interconnected and operated on a coordinated basis to achieve economies in supplying combined loads.

price squeeze: the establishment of a retail rate lower than the wholesale rate by a wholesale seller that is in competition for retail sales with its wholesale customers.

promotional rate: a rate form that promotes the sale of electricity by encouraging additional purchases of electricity through reduced unit costs.

rate forms:
    declining block rates: a rate which provides for declining unit costs with increasing usage of demand or energy.
    lifeline rate: a rate for a specified level of usage, usually for residential service, at a less than fully allocated cost.
    interruptible rate: a rate for service which the utility may interrupt at its own discretion to protect its load.
    peak period rates: rates with higher charges for demand and energy at the time of the system peak; developed on a seasonal or a daily peak basis (time-of-day).

wheeling service: use of the transmission facilities of one system to transmit the power of another system.

INTRODUCTION

On April 20, 1977, President Carter addressed a joint session of Congress outlining principles of policy, strategies, and goals embodied in the administration's National Energy Plan. Of ten enumerated national energy policy principles, three will directly affect the rates of the electric utility industry. These three principles are: protection of the environment through the avoidance of wasteful use of resources; reduction of energy demand through conservation; and pricing energy at its replacement cost.[1] In addition, the National Energy Plan adopts as a goal a reduction in the rate of growth of demand to less than 2 percent a year and the conversion of utilities and industry to the use of coal and other abundant fuels instead of oil and gas.

As part of the overall program, the President proposed the reform of electric utility rate structures and ratemaking. This reform is based on the assumption that conventional utility pricing policies discourage conservation, since small users pay the highest unit price while larger users get the benefit of declining block rates. The reforms further assume that current rates do not reflect the costs imposed in producing electricity, resulting in waste and inequity.[2] The administration legislation proposes, therefore, the elimination of promotional and declining block rates that do not reflect costs; the shift of electric energy use to off-peak periods through time-of-day and peak-period prices and interruptible rate schedules; the prohibition of master metering; and authorizing the Federal Power Commission to require interconnection, power pooling, and wheeling. The legislation would also encourage cogeneration by requiring fair rates for the sale of power by and to cogenerators. The Federal Power Commission would also have jurisdiction to order utilities to interconnect with cogenerators. The Federal Energy Administration is to prescribe rules under which utilities are to offer to purchase from and sell to cogenerators.[3]

Concern with electric utility pricing practices has arisen independently of the concern for a comprehensive national energy policy. During the first two-thirds of this century, electric utility costs and rates generally declined. Marginal and average costs of the utilities have declined because of economies of scale resulting from the natural monopoly of the electric utilities and improved technology. However, in the late 1960s and early 1970s, this trend was dramatically reversed, and the electric utility industry has been required, with increasing frequency, to seek rate increases before the state and federal authorities with jurisdiction over such rates. These increases have been attributable to a number of factors: a reduction in the economies of scale to the industry; inflation, particularly in interest, capital costs, and the cost of building new capacity; delay in the building of new plants, sometimes because of successful energy conservation by consumers; and, since 1973, dramatic increases in the cost of fuel to generate electric energy. This paper will address the electric rate reform sections of the National Energy Act, H.R.

3

8444, introduced by Rep. Ashley (D-Ohio). It was passed by the House on August 5, 1977, and incorporates not only the proposals of the administration bill but also certain other proposals introduced by others in this session and in the 94th Congress. This paper will also consider the administration's bill, introduced by Sen. Jackson (D-Wash.), which is presently pending in the Senate as S.1469.

BACKGROUND: EXISTING REGULATION

Sales of electric energy by investor-owned utilities are currently subject to a dual system of regulation in most jurisdictions. Local distribution and retail sales of electricity are generally and historically subject to local regulation by state commission or municipal authority. In 1927, the Supreme Court, in the case of *Public Utilities Comm'n* v. *Attleboro Steam & Electric Co.,* held that wholesale sales of electricity in interstate commerce were outside the authority of state commissions to regulate.[4] This "Attleboro gap," as it was called, was filled by the passage of the Public Utility Act of 1935. This act changed the Federal Water Power Act (41 Stat. 1063, 16 U.S.C. 791-823) by making that earlier act Part I of the new Federal Power Act and enacting new Parts II and III thereof (16 U.S.C. 824-825R).

Utility regulatory commissions are generally charged, among other things, with regulation of rates and charges for service by electric utilities. Most regulatory statutes require that rates and charges shall be just and reasonable and not unduly discriminatory or preferential. In addition to rate-setting authority, commissions are often vested with certificate and franchise authority, jurisdiction over financial transactions and the issuance of securities, and jurisdiction over any other practices which may affect electric service in the jurisdiction. The Federal Power Commission, in addition to its jurisdiction over sales of electricity for resale in interstate commerce, also has authority over issuance of securities when this subject is not regulated by the states. The Federal Power Commission may also provide for voluntary interconnections and in certain circumstances may require such interconnections.

For many years utility regulation was concerned with the valuation of property subject to utility commission jurisdiction. In the case of *Smyth* v. *Ames,* 169 U.S. 466 (1898), the Supreme Court indicated various concepts of valuation of investment in the enterprise which must be taken into consideration in setting utility rates. In the landmark case of *FPC* v. *Hope Natural Gas Co.,* 320 U.S. 593 (1944), the Supreme Court held that, under a statute without a formula for the establishment of just and reasonable rates, it is the result reached and not the method used that determines the validity of a commission's rate order.[5] In this opinion, the "original cost" method of rate-base determination was also upheld. This method has consistently been used by the Federal Power Commission and many state commissions since that time.[6] The just and reasonable standard of the Natural Gas Act interpreted in *Hope* is common to most utility rate statutes and is identical to the rate standards of the Federal Power Act, under which the Federal Power Commission regulates interstate wholesale sales of electricity.

Historically, rate regulation has been concerned with the protection of consumers against monopoly profits. Generally, rates are established on the basis of the historic cost of providing service over a given period of time. From these historic costs, commissions determine the representative cost of rendering the service within the commission's jurisdiction. Permissible costs include operating and maintenance expenses, depreciation, and taxes.

The utility is also entitled to a return on its investment. This return includes the cost of debt as well as a fair return on equity invested in the enterprise.[7] Under orginal-cost–rate-base regulation, a fair rate-of-return percentage is derived, and this figure is then multiplied times the rate base to determine the overall return dollars allowed.[8]

In an original cost jurisdiction, the major components of rate base are the original cost of plant in service that is deemed used and useful in the public interest, less accumulated reserves for depreciation, plus an allowance for working capital and certain prepayments. There may be minor variations in these components between jurisdictions. For example, the Federal Power Commission has recently issued a rule permitting the inclusion in electric utility rate base of construction work in progress related to pollution control equipment.[9] This rule is a departure from traditional regulation at the FPC. Under certain circumstances, research and development expenditures may also be included in rate base.[10]

After revenue requirements are determined, costs must be allocated and rates designed in order to permit the utility the opportunity to recover its cost of service. Costs may be allocated to services using a myriad of factors. One analyst has identified at least twenty-nine methods of allocating peak responsibility costs.[11] Costs must be allocated to customers in the jurisdiction subject to regulation by the commission and to customers not subject to that commission's jurisdiction. The costs allocated to jurisdictional customers must then be allocated among customers and classes of customers. Rates are then designed to recover allocated costs from each customer and customer class.

Most utility regulatory statutes prohibit undue discrimination between classes of service. Courts have interpreted this provision as permitting differences in rates based on differences in costs.[12] Commissions have permitted subsidization of one class of consumers by another when such results were considered in the public interest and therefore not undue discrimination.[13] Thus, sales to one consumer class at less than fully allocated costs may bring economies of scale and resulting benefits to all classes of customers, while avoiding unnecessary duplication of facilities. If the subsidized class pays all of the variable costs of the service plus a fraction of the fixed costs, the costs to be paid by all other customers are to that extent lower.

Since the trend of increasing costs began and the utilities commenced seeking increased rates on a regular basis, the subjects of cost allocation and rate design have become increasingly significant in state and federal jurisdictions. The principles of cost allocation and rate design require a separation of the cost incurred into fixed costs and variable costs. The cost of providing electric service comprises demand, energy, and customer costs. These costs must be allocated to a consumer or class of consumers in a fair and equitable manner based on the incidence of cost in supplying that class of service. Rates must then be designed which will fairly allocate the burdens of providing the utility service to the consumers receiving the service.[14]

Traditionally, electric utility rates have been designed as declining block rates, with rates for certain classes of customers separated into two or even three parts. Residential rates are generally one-part declining block rates. Industrial rates are generally on a two- or three-part basis, with separate demand and energy charges and in some cases a customer charge. Under two-part rates, both demand and energy charges are generally of a declining block nature. These rates are designed to recover the customer and demand or capacity costs in the initial higher blocks, while the rates in the tail blocks recover the variable energy costs of providing additional service.[15]

Many utility commissions have begun to flatten the declining block rates or to eliminate them altogether, raising the presumption that declining block rates are not cost justified or are *prima facie* unduly discriminatory.[16] Furthermore, commissions have been experimenting with marginal cost determinations for purposes of establishing rates.[17] Many state utility commissions have recently required a lifeline rate for residential service.[18] These rates are intended to provide an essential level of service for the beneficiary class, usually identified as the poor or the elderly. This rate is generally based on a minimum level of usage, such as 300 kilowatt-hours per month.[19] Under lifeline rates, utilities are permitted to recover the difference between the lifeline rate and the cost of that service by charging a higher rate to other rate payers.[20]

Under the Federal Power Act, the Federal Power Commission has jurisdiction over sales for resale in interstate commerce and over the transmission of electric energy in interstate commerce. The Federal Power Act requires that rates for resale are to be just, reasonable, and nondiscriminatory. The commission, in order to assure an abundant supply of energy, may divide the country into districts for voluntary interconnection, and is required to promote such interconnection and coordination. The Federal Power Commission may order an interconnection between utilities under certain conditions.[21]

Recently, the Supreme Court has affirmed that the Federal Power Commission has jurisdiction to consider whether retail rates are set by a utility at a lower level than its wholesale rates in order to effect a price squeeze against a utility's wholesale customer.[22] The Federal Power Commission, although it has limited interconnection jurisdiction, does not have the authority to compel a utility to wheel power across its transmission facilities from a supplier to the supplier's nonconnected customer.[23] Nor does the Federal Power Commission have extensive authority to require interconnection and power pooling, since the act is premised on voluntary business transactions, not compulsion by the Federal Power Commission.[24]

7

MAJOR ELECTRIC RATE REFORM BILLS

Several major bills which would reform electric utility ratemaking were introduced in Congress during the Second Session of the 94th Congress and again in the First Session of the 95th Congress. H.R. 6660, proposed by Rep. Dingell (D-Mich.), and the administration bill, H.R. 6831, proposed by Rep. Wright (D-Tex.), were the most comprehensive bills introduced. The bills were considered by the Ad Hoc Committee on Energy, established to consider energy proposals from the various standing committees of the House. The Ad Hoc Committee bill, H.R. 8444, proposed by Rep. Ashley (D-Ohio), was substantially adopted by the House on August 5, 1977. The administration bill is pending in the Senate as S. 1469, proposed by Sen. Jackson (D-Wash.). There are many provisions common to the House bill and the Senate bill, but the House bill has more extensive and specific provisions concerning the common components, as well as provisions not covered by the Senate bill.

Provisions Common to
the House Bill and the Senate Bill

Cost of Service.   State agencies are required to prescribe one or more methods for determining the cost of providing electric service. These methods are required to reflect differences in cost incurrence based on daily and seasonal time of use. They must also take into account the extent to which costs are likely to change if a consumer (defined as any person or agency to whom electricity is sold, other than for resale), or a class of consumers, causes additional capacity to be added to meet the system peak, or causes additional kilowatt hours to be delivered. In the event, states do not prescribe the methods; the Federal Power Commission (House bill) or Federal Energy Administration (Senate bill) is to prescribe these methods.

Utilities are required to gather data to show consumption patterns, the causes of changes in daily and seasonal peaks, and the cost of serving consumer classes.

Rate Design.   State agencies are to assure that utilities will comply with defined national policies. Rates shall be designed to reflect costs; however, rates do not reflect costs if the rate per kilowatt-hour decreases as consumption increases. Rates are also to be based on seasonal and time-of-day differences in costs. Utilities are to provide load management systems. Industrial and commercial customers shall be offered an interruptible rate. Nothing in the act prohibits a rate lower than a cost-based rate for residential needs. Master metered service is to be prohibited.

States have two years to demonstrate that they are implementing the policy of the act.

The utilities are required to report the implementation of the rate design policies. The federal authorities (the Federal Power Commission under the House bill, the Federal Energy Administration under S. 1469) are empowered to determine whether a utility is in compliance with the national policies. If they find that the utility is not in compliance they have authority to require implementation through the prohibition of rate increases until compliance with the national policies is determined.

Interconnection and Wheeling.   Section 202(b) of the Federal Power Act is amended to permit the Federal Power Commission to order physical connection of transmission facilities of a utility with another utility, or cogenerator, and the sale and delivery of energy to, coordination with, and wheeling for, the utility or cogenerator. Rules are to be promulgated requiring utilities to offer to sell electricity to cogenerators and to purchase from them, both at rates that do not discriminate against cogenerators. Section 202(a) is amended to delete the word *voluntary* from the Federal Power Commission's authority to require interconnection.

Differences between
the House Bill and the Senate Bill

There are many differences between the House bill and the Senate bill. These differences relate to policy implementation as well as details of coverage of the common provisions. Major differences are described below.

Rate Design Differences.   The House bill prohibits declining block rates for capacity charges and for energy charges, while the Senate bill prohibits declining block rates only for energy charges. However, under the House bill, declining block rates may be approved if the utility demonstrates, in an evidentiary hearing, that declining block rates reflect a decrease in the cost of service to the consumer as consumption increases.

The House bill requires time-of-day rates unless such rates are determined not to be cost effective (cost effective is defined for purposes of time-of-day rates only if the long-run benefits are likely to exceed the metering costs). If time-of-day rates are not cost effective, the utility is to offer such rates to consumers willing to pay the metering costs. Under the Senate bill, utilities are required to offer time-of-day rates to consumers willing to pay the metering costs. The cost-effective standard is also applied to seasonal rates under the House bill, but, for this purpose, the standard is not defined. If this undefined standard is met, rates must be set on a seasonal basis. Under the Senate bill, utilities are required only to offer seasonal rates.

Additional Major Provisions
of the House Bill

Rate Design and Cost of Service.   The bill establishes standards regarding advertising and detailed rules on what costs associated with such advertising may be passed on to the consumer in rates for electric service. Promotional advertising and political or institutional advertising are excluded from recovery from consumers. If such expenses are recovered from consumers, the utility is deemed not in compliance with the rate design mandates of the act.

The House bill deals extensively with automatic adjustment clauses for state regulated retail rates and wholesale rates subject to Federal Power Commission jurisdiction. The act provides that there shall be no increase in rates prior to hearing, except under qualifying automatic adjustment clauses. A qualifying automatic adjustment clause must provide incentives for efficient use of resources, including economic purchase and use of fuel, and must be necessary to enable a utility to meet any short-term financial obligations. Adjustments may also reflect increases in the cost of power purchased from a centrally dispatched power pool. These clauses are required to be reviewed by the state commission or Federal Power Commission every two years and must be the subject of an evidentiary hearing every four years. The review of these clauses is to consist of examination and an audit, if necessary, of the utility practices subject to the clause.

No rate increase is permitted to become effective if it is not in compliance with the rate design standards of the act. No determination of compliance with minimum standards of rate design can be made unless the authority with jurisdiction has made a finding concerning causes of changes in peak load, both daily and seasonal, and the cost of serving a consumer class and of serving different consumption patterns (voltage and time based). Annual capital, operating, and maintenance costs are to be separately reported for each generating unit and for transmission and distribution services. The determination of compliance must further be based on the cost determination methods prescribed pursuant to this section. For utilities without lifeline rates, the regulatory authority is to determine whether such rates should be implemented. The various jurisdictions will be free, except as to advertising expenses noted above, to devise their own methods of prescribing cost of service.

Wholesale Rate Reform.   The Federal Power Commission must make its decision on increased wholesale rates (subject to its jurisdiction) within ten months of the original filing of the increased rate schedule. "Pancaking" of rate increases, that is, the filing of an increase on top of an increase which has not been decided by the Federal Power Commission, is prohibited. If the Federal Power Commission has not decided a case within ten months, the commission loses its authority to decide the case. The chairman of the commission is then required to decide the case by a final order within two additional months. The definition of a lawful rate is expanded to include, in addition to the just and reasonable standard, the requirement that rates are to be otherwise lawful. If differences between wholesale rates and retail rates are unreasonable or anticompetitive, a rate is not lawful. The commission is also granted authority to prohibit unfair methods of competition and to reject filings that would result in unfair methods of competition.

RATE DESIGN AND
COST OF SERVICE REFORM

The reforms with the greatest rate impact on utilities and consumers are the required changes in retail rate design and cost-of-service determinations. While economists have long urged the microeconomic theory that all goods should be priced at their marginal cost in order to best allocate society's resources, the industry and commissions regulating it have been reluctant to adopt this concept.[25] Most recent electric utility rate reform recommendations have favored some form of marginal cost pricing for electricity and both the House-passed bill and the administration bill pending in the Senate embody this recommendation.

Arguments in Favor
of Electric Rate Reform

Arguments for Rate Design Reforms. Various commentators have criticized declining block rates as based on an outmoded principle—that electric utilities are still in a situation of increasing economies of scale with resulting declining unit costs.[26] One reform bill introduced in the House, H.R. 6009 proposed by Rep. Allen (D-Tenn.), specifically embodied this criticism in its findings:

> (3) the existing inequitable electric rate schedules, particularly as they include quantity discount rates and declining block rates, that generally prevail throughout the electric utility industry, result in some classes of consumers paying less than their fair share of the cost of the service they receive, including the high cost of increasing generating, plant, and transmission capacity needed to meet electric energy demands during peak-load periods, and such inequitable rate schedules thereby encourage the wasteful use of electric energy and other limited natural resources of the Nation;

These criticisms are based on various factors with the ultimate conclusion that declining block rates are no longer justified on the basis of costs. In order to conserve energy or to allocate resources perfectly, electricity should be priced at its marginal cost.[27]

Even during periods of declining costs, marginal cost pricing has been suggested by many economists in order to allocate resources better. A criticism of marginal cost pricing recognized at that time was that this method of pricing would not provide revenues equal to the cost of providing the utility service. As a remedy for this deficiency, rates in excess of marginal costs would be established for the class of customer whose usage would change least with a change in rate. This proposal has been labeled the inverse elasticity rule.

Marginal cost pricing and inverse elasticity are also applicable for periods when costs are increasing. Thus, when rates are set at a marginal cost which exceeds average costs, revenues would be in excess of the revenue requirements needed to provide the service, unjustly enriching the utility. The class of customers with the lowest elasticity of demand would receive a rate less than the marginal cost in order to prevent excess revenues.[28]

Since most utilities have experienced economies of scale and resulting declining unit costs over most yardsticks for measurement, declining block rates were historically acceptable to most parties. Critics now suggest that this represents a subsidization of large users within any class by smaller users within that class. In *Madison Gas & Electric* [29] rates were flattened on the theory that declining block rates were no longer cost justified. Several other jurisdictions have reached this same result.[30]

Seasonal rates have also been generally proposed as a form of peak-load pricing in order to promote efficient allocation of resources. Most utilities are either summer-peaking or winter-peaking utilities. As a consequence, installed capacity must be greater to provide service during the peak season. When peak-season rates are higher than off-season rates, economists believe that consumption decisions will be modified, over time, to reduce the seasonal peak demand on the utility and consequent generation capacity needed.[31]

Environmentalists have suggested inverted rates, rather than flat rates, with the rate increasing with usage. This rate design is intended to discourage the sale of electricity and to internalize external costs with resulting benefits in saving fuel, reducing pollution, and avoiding the building of additional high-cost capacity.[32]

Time-of-day rates have also been suggested as a means of assessing the cost of the service to the user responsible for cost, while promoting efficient resource allocation and preventing waste. Since capacity is not added in discrete increments, but in large blocks, the increase in peak demand which calls forth additional capacity is identified as the cause of cost incurrence on a utility system. Furthermore, utility operations are such that large, efficient, base-load generators are designed to operate continuously throughout the year. These base-load units have high capital costs but low fuel costs. Intermediate and peaking units have decreasing capital costs but are increasingly inefficient and therefore have higher fuel costs. Most utilities plan to have available reserve capacity equal to the capacity of the largest unit in the event of forced outage. Thus, the cost of providing capacity and energy at the time of the system peak is greatest. Users at the time of the system peak should therefore be charged the costs of providing this service. A consumer's choice to consume electricity would be based on knowledge of the true cost of the product, and resources would be efficiently allocated. Under this theory, off-peak capacity is a joint product of peak capacity and therefore should bear none of the capacity costs. Off-peak energy sales would be priced to recover only the variable costs (mainly fuel) of producing a kilowatt-hour during off-peak periods.[33]

14

One proponent of time-of-day rates has identified ten specific benefits they provide:

- cost minimization to the utility
- equity in the tariff
- maximization of social welfare and economic efficiency
- load factor improvement
- reduced external costs
- energy conservation
- earnings stability
- tariff stability
- consumer benefit
- industrial protection[34]

Lifeline rates have been advocated as a means of providing an essential level of electric service, generally for a class of consumers such as the poor or the elderly on fixed incomes. Lifeline rates will insulate the benefited class of consumer from increases in the cost of essential electric needs.[35]

Promotional and institutional advertising expenses are excluded from a utility's cost of service on the theory that these expenses are of no benefit to the consumer. Recently, one commission thoroughly discussed the reasons for this exclusion.[36] The obvious reason to prohibit promotional advertising is to limit growth, particularly in peak demand. However, advertising to promote off-peak use to increase load factor was also banned since off-peak loads consume primary fuels and contribute to pollution. Furthermore, promotion of off-peak season uses like heat pumps, or other methods of electric space heat, will, with the addition of central air conditioning, contribute to the summer system peak. With increasing costs, there is therefore no benefit of increased economies of scale to the consumer from increased sales resulting from promotional advertising.

Political and institutional advertising were viewed as in the self-interest of management and shareholders and therefore not a proper expense to be borne by ratepayers. This exclusion of advertising was successfully defended against a claim that commercial speech is protected by the First Amendment guarantee of freedom of speech, since there is a legitimate state concern in preventing the increased costs, pollution, and use of resources which would result from increased sales. Furthermore, the commission pointed out that it was not prohibiting the expression of a position, but merely prohibiting the cost from being passed on to the ratepayer.

Automatic adjustment clauses have been criticized because they do not permit review before charges are increased to ratepayers. Further, they are said to provide no incentive for economic operation of the utility, since increased costs are automatically recovered.[37] Thus, the act would require stringent reporting and review requirements, as well as findings that the automatic adjustment clause operated to provide an incentive for efficient operation.[38]

Arguments for Other Provisions.   One of the specific purposes of the House bill is "to increase the efficiency of generation, transmission, and distribution of electric power through encouragement of competition."[39] This is also one of the important parts of the administration program.[40] The Supreme Court has recognized the advantages of interconnection to an isolated system.[41] It has also recognized that refusal to wheel and a refusal to sell wholesale power are a means of preventing retail competition.[42] However, existing regulatory law is based on voluntary commercial relationships and not regulatory control.[43] Both the House and the Senate bills greatly expand Federal Power Commission authority and permit it to require wheeling, sale of power, coordination, and power pooling. This expansion of authority is seen as essential to permit retail competition, particularly by publicly owned systems in competition with private (investor-owned) systems.[44]

The Supreme Court rejected arguments that a compulsion to provide wheeling will result in deterioration of the investor-owned utilities. The Court stated that the antitrust laws assume "that an enterprise will protect itself against loss by operating with superior service, lower costs, and increased efficiency."[45] Therefore, improper methods of competition should be prohibited. The bills therefore change the regulatory scheme to give the Federal Power Commission authority to implement wheeling, a power not previously granted. The acts further expand the Federal Power Commission authority to provide regulatory direction over interconnection and coordination, a field previously left to private arrangements.

The antipancaking amendment to the Federal Power Act is further seen as a benefit to competition. The ability of a wholesale seller to file a rate increase with the Federal Power Commission and have it take effect after a thirty-day notice period, and with a maximum suspension of five months,[46] has been seen as facilitating a price squeeze,[47] since the utility would be permitted to charge a rate that had not been determined to be lawful. There is also no present limitation on the right to file additional rate increases before a pending case is decided. Under the House bill, it has been argued, wholesale purchasers are protected from a price squeeze as a result of an unlawful rate taking effect, subject to refund, or from the pancaking of rate filings.[48]

The existing remedy for a prohibited price squeeze, is the establishment of a wholesale rate at the lower boundary of the zone of reasonableness,[49] but, it is argued that this will not cure the discrimination inherent in having different levels of rates for wholesale and retail sales.[50] While an antitrust action is available,[51] the act will grant the Federal Power Commission authority to prohibit unfair trade practices through rejection of a filing, or by an order. The Federal Power Commission has previously asserted jurisdiction over unfair practices resulting from contracts required to be on file with the commission, and practices affecting those contracts.[52]

Arguments against
Electric Rate Reform

Arguments against Rate Design Reforms. Criticisms of the rate design reforms proposed by both bills are of a general and specific nature. The most frequently leveled criticism against rate reform proposals is that they are based on economic theory but not the cost of utility service.[53] Furthermore, critics suggest that to the extent reform is necessary, it is presently being implemented at the state level, where consideration of differences in the needs of the consumers, utilities, and general welfare of the jurisdiction may be considered, whereas a federally mandated program will foreclose the local diversity necessary to protect local needs.[54] Specific criticisms of the various proposals go to each aspect of the proposed reforms.

Criticism of the prohibition of declining block rates is most often based on the theory that costs decrease as usage increases.[55] There are costs associated with service to each customer (for example, carrying charges on investment in the distribution system necessary to serve the customer, meter reading, billing, and other general overhead). Initial blocks of rates are designed to recover these costs plus the cost of producing the energy consumed in the initial block. After the customer costs are recovered, the remaining blocks may be set lower, since the costs to be recovered are only the cost of the energy supplied. Service to large users is cheaper, since fixed costs are spread over more units of output, and therefore the rates for higher use should be lower. Service to industrial customers taking service at transmission-level voltages is significantly cheaper than service to residential users which requires investment in transformers and a distribution system.[56]

Seasonal pricing is criticized because it may result in needle peaks, which are even less efficient in allocating resources than the same overall seasonal peak with better load factor. These needle peaks occur because the elasticity of demand among consumers may be great. For instance, for a summer-peaking system, elasticity of demand for electric air conditioning on 80 degree days will be great and usage will be discouraged on those days. However, the elasticity of demand may disappear as the humidity increases and the temperature rises over 90 degrees.[57] Accordingly, the same capacity will be required on those very hot days, with less efficient use being made of a utility's generation capability because of a lower load factor. In the past, utilities promoted off-peak usage in order to increase customer load factor, thereby spreading fixed costs over greater units of sales. However, additional sales off-peak consume primary resources and may ultimately lead to a shift in the system peak. If the peak shifts, capacity may have to be built to serve a former off-peak period, which becomes a new system peak. Also, the imposition of load which otherwise might not be served during off-peak periods may cause a modification in required off-peak capacity in order that scheduled maintenance may be performed with sufficient capacity remaining to serve off-peak load.[58] Seasonal rates are not justifiable for utilities whose seasonal peaks "leap frog" (that is, each seasonal peak exceeds the immediately preceding seasonal peak) since the seasonal rate would not limit the capacity needed to meet the succeeding off-season load.[59]

Time-of-day rates are criticized primarily because of the cost of metering each consumer to provide the measurement of demand at the time of peak use.[60] There are more costs involved in providing time-of-day service than just metering, since bills must be rendered, rate schedules provided, and analyses made. One analyst has criticized the provision of such time-of-day rates on a voluntary basis because that may cause some, and then all, customers to switch to this rate even though the overall benefits to the utility and society may not be cost effective in the first place. This result obtains when an individual may benefit from the rate, without a commensurate benefit to the utility or to all customers. After one customer, who benefits because of a price advantage, takes advantage of this individual benefit, the greater remaining costs must be recovered from consumers who do not change to time-of-day rates. Accordingly, charges for customers who have not changed to time-of-day rates must increase, leading to the same result as an individual switch based on individual advantage. This process repeats until all consumers switch, although, collectively, time-of-day rates as a whole do not benefit the consumers of the utility.[61]

Furthermore, the overall composition of load, not just the peak, is seen as cost determinative. Therefore, pricing on a time-of-day basis does not accurately assess costs to all customers.[62] The Federal Power Commission, in allocating pipeline transmission costs (capacity costs), historically has allocated one-half of these capacity costs on a volumetric, rather than peak-use, basis. This prohibits off-peak use from getting a "free ride" by avoiding capacity costs.[63]

The further effect time-of-day pricing may have on working patterns in industry is uncertain, but reports indicate that, where time-of-day pricing has been imposed, users are increasing night-shift work.[64] Commercial customers would be unable to take advantage of off-peak rates, since they are restricted by ordinary business hours and living habits.[65] In any event, where businesses are unable to take advantage of off-peak rates, increases in the cost of electricity will inevitably be reflected in an increased cost of goods.

Most proponents of lifeline rates either identify the class of consumer that subsidizes the lifeline service or rely on the "inverse elasticity rule." However, under the House bill, all rates except the lifeline rates are to be cost based. This result raises the possibility that shareholders, and not other consumers, would be required to subsidize consumers using lifeline rates.[66] While individual rates are not required to produce net revenues, they must be set at a level which permits the utility to recover costs, including capital costs.[67] Furthermore, many analysts have cited problems, particularly with the definitions involved in lifeline rate proposals, even when a subsidy is permitted under the statute or decisions. A widely used cutoff point for lifeline rates is 300 kilowatt-hours per month, the amount which can be used by an electric water heater alone. When the difference between cost and revenues is collected from nonlifeline residential customers and lifeline customers using over 300 kilowatt-hours, the intended beneficiary could end up paying more.[68] Further problems exist for persons who pay rent which includes their utility bills. They would receive no benefit from lifeline rates. In addition, the benefits of lifeline electric rates would accrue solely to electric utility customers and would provide no relief for the poor, the elderly, or other residential customers who use natural gas, fuel oil, or other means for cooking, heating, cooling, or other home uses.[69]

Many economists and analysts favoring rate reform oppose a lifeline rate type of subsidy. Economists believe that subsidies should be clearly identified as such. Generally, most regard public utilities and utility commissions as ill-suited for such income redistribution and welfare-related activities. Rather, these critics believe that the cost to each consumer should be based on the cost of providing service to that consumer. For income redistribution purposes, a program like utility or fuel stamps or other direct governmental subsidies would provide the same result for all persons in the beneficiary class, not just for electric consumers, while the efficient economic information from electric rates would be provided to all consumers.[70]

Of the many operating and maintenance expenses incurred by electric utilities, advertising expenses are singled out for detailed rules on the costs that may be passed on to the consumer in their rates for electric service. Opponents of this prohibition have criticized the restrictions as being concerned with a *de minimis* amount of expense. These opponents have also expressed concern over electricity's role in providing the energy needs in the market as a whole and the function that promotional and institutional advertising plays. Other forms of energy would not have similar restraints and would therefore have an undue advantage over electricity. Furthermore, critics claim that this prohibition infringes the rights of freedom of speech.[71] Opponents of these restrictions argue that the issues discussed in utility advertising are of great social significance, and the utilities' views should be freely expressed in order that there be a full public discussion of important issues.[72]

Opponents of the current legislation argue that the operation of automatic adjustment clauses is inherently to level rates and is therefore in conformity with the prohibition against declining block rates. To the extent these clauses are discouraged, this rate-flattening provision will be lost.

The proposed conditions attendant to the use of these clauses has been criticized as being unduly restrictive, since a utility may not be able to show the necessity of the clause to meet immediate financial obligations. Since fuel prices for the future may soar, regulatory lag would prevent implementation of a fuel clause when it was necessary to meet financial obligations. In addition, any decrease in costs would not be passed on to the consumer in the absence of an automatic adjustment clause. The review, audit, and hearing proceedings have also been criticized as being burdensome and a tool for harassment.[73]

The Federal Power Commission has recently issued a notice of proposed rulemaking concerning the public availability of data concerning fuel costs reported to the Federal Power Commission. Under the rule, these data would be available only to federal and state government officials for a period of one year. This rule would be contrary to the House bill, which would permit consumers complete access to the books of the utilities. The rationale for limiting disclosure is that the availability of the fuel price data would permit price fixing by fuel suppliers.[74]

Arguments against Other Provisions. The expansion of Federal Power Commission authority to require interconnection, wheeling, and coordination has been criticized because much of this activity is currently being carried out on a voluntary basis. Further, an investor-owned utility could be required to sell power to a public power agency under conditions prejudicial to customers of the investor-owned utility. Opponents argue that wheeling would lead to "cream skimming" of profitable loads and misallocation of resources through subsidies to nontaxed public systems.[75] One utility representative considered the interconnection authority to be counterproductive, leading to fragmentation of the industry into small, inefficient systems instead of the large, efficient systems which result from voluntary actions. Investor-owned utilities, which pay taxes to state and federal jurisdictions, should not be required to compete for sales with municipal utilities that pay no taxes and then be required to transmit power generated by a tax-exempt utility to the investor-owned company's customer/competitor. The commission's authority would also be extended to transactions of an intrastate nature. Furthermore, opponents state that under the new powers, the Federal Power Commission would replace utility management in the operation of the utility's activities, a first step toward nationalization of the industry.[76] In the *Otter Tail* litigation, the company argued that the requirement that it interconnect and wheel could ultimately lead to its downfall.

General Federal Power Commission jurisdiction over unfair trade practices has also been subjected to criticism since that commission does not have antitrust expertise. The broadness of the "unfair competition" standard has been criticized as being without limitation and subject to abuse. The unfair competition provision, together with the price-squeeze provision, could lead to obstruction of necessary rate relief.[77]

ADDITIONAL PROVISIONS

The House bill would provide for increased participation by electric consumers in retail rate proceedings, with the consumers allowed to collect their fees and costs from the utilities if the consumer prevails in a ratemaking proceeding. The act further amends the Federal Power Act to provide for an office of public counsel to be created at the Federal Power Commission for purposes of, among other things, appearing in rate case proceedings and to compensate intervenors in proceedings at the Federal Power Commission.[78] These provisions have been criticized as being unnecessary since consumers are now represented in rate proceedings. The provision may also be subject to abuse by special interests not interested in rate regulation but opposed to energy development in general and hoping to create further regulatory lag.[79]

The Federal Power Commission would also be given authority to assure continuity of service to retail and wholesale customers and to require that any plan to cope with a shortage of energy be developed in a nondiscriminatory manner between wholesale and retail customers. This provision has been criticized because a wholesale purchaser who benefits from tax advantages and other subsidies may indirectly encourage high consumption of electricity because of lower rates. Therefore, energy shortages can be the fault of wholesale rather than retail customers.[80]

The act would also provide for rules concerning electric utility reliability. Such rules are to consider the minimization of costs and expenses but also may require minimum standards of quality in bulk power facilities. This provision has been criticized because reliability is based on the unique needs of a particular system and, also, on the possibility that the Federal Power Commission, instead of utility management, would assume authority over reliability.[81]

21

NOTES TO TEXT

[1] The White House, Detailed Fact Sheet, *The President's Energy Program*, April 20, 1977, p. 1.

[2] *The President's Energy Program*, p. 10.

[3] Ibid., pp. 9-10.

[4] 273 U.S. 83 (1927).

[5] This opinion dealt with regulation under the Natural Gas Act (15 U.S.C. 717), which prohibits unjust, unreasonable, unduly discriminatory, and preferential rates.

[6] The Federal Power Commission determined that thirty-two states employ the original cost method, while the rest use other methods such as "fair value" or "reproduction cost." Federal Power Commission, *Federal and State Commission Jurisdiction and Regulation of Electric, Gas, and Telephone Utilities*, 1973, p. 21.

[7] Bluefield Water Works & Improvement Co. v. Public Service Commission, 262 U.S. 679 (1923); FPC v. Hope Natural Gas Co., 320 U.S. 591 (1944).

[8] J. C. Bonbright, *Principles of Public Utility Rates* (New York: Columbia University Press, 1961); Alfred E. Kahn, *The Economics of Regulation* (New York: John Wiley & Sons, Inc., 1970), vol. 1.

[9] Order No. 555, Docket No. RM75-13 (Nov. 8, 1976). The Federal Power Commission's Regulations were amended to include a new regulation, 18 C.F.R. 2.100.

[10] 18 C.F.R. 35.22.

[11] Bonbright, *Principles of Public Utility Rates*, p. 351.

[12] St. Michael's Utilities Commission v. FPC, 377 F.2d 912 (1967).

[13] Southwestern Public Service Co., 33 FPC 343 (1965). This is also embodied in the concept of lifeline rates embodied in both bills.

[14] Kahn, *Economics of Regulation*, and Bonbright, *Principles of Public Utility Rates*.

[15] Louis Flax and Mark Drazen, *Current Proposals for Changes in the Design of Electric Utility Rates* (Washington, D.C.: National Association of Manufacturers, 1976).

[16] Detroit Edison Co., 3 P.U.R. 4th 209 (Michigan Public Service Commission, 1974); Consolidated Edison Co. of New York, 8 P.U.R. 4th 475 (New York Public Service

Commission, 1975); Madison Gas & Electric Co., 5 P.U.R. 4th 28 (Wisconsin Public Service Commission, 1974).

[17] Madison Gas & Electric, 5 P.U.R.4th 28.

[18] In 1976, the National Association of Regulatory Utility Commissioners (NARUC), in *Lifeline Rates* (1976), identified five jurisdictions with such rates.

[19] NARUC, *Lifeline Rates,* p. 50.

[20] Ibid.

[21] Gainesville Utilities Dept. v. Florida Power Corp., 402 U.S. 515 (1971).

[22] FPC v. Conway Corp., 426 U.S. 271 (1976).

[23] Otter Tail Power Co. v. United States, 410 U.S. 366, 375 (1973).

[24] Ibid., pp. 373-74.

[25] Paul A. Samuelson, *Economics, An Introductory Analysis,* fifth edition (New York: McGraw Hill, 1971), pp. 411-543; Edward Berlin, Charles Cicchetti, William Giller, *Perspectives on Power* (Cambridge, Massachusetts: Ballinger Publishing Co., 1974).

[26] Samuel Huntington, "The Rapid Emergence of Marginal Cost Pricing in the Regulation of Electric Utility Rate Structures," *Boston University Law Review,* vol. 55 (1975), pp. 689-722; Carolyn Brancato, "New Approaches to Current Problems in Electric Utility Rate Reform," *Columbia Journal of Environmental Law,* vol. 2 (1975), p. 40.

[27] Brancato, "New Approaches," p. 47.

[28] Other methods suggested to make up the revenue deficiency (or surplus) are by external subsidy or taxation, although these methods are recognized to be outside the authority of the regulatory commission. Gary Grainger, "A Practical Approach to Peak Day Pricing," *Public Utilities Fortnightly,* September 9, 1976, p. 19.

[29] 5 P.U.R.4th 83.

[30] Berlin et al., *Perspectives on Power,* p. 66, identifies thirteen utilities or jurisdictions which have acted to flatten block rates.

[31] Kahn, *Economics of Regulation,* pp. 89-103.

[32] Brancato, "New Approaches"; Kahn, *Economics of Regulation,* p. 193.

[33] Paul L. Joskow, *"Applying Economic Principles to Public Utility Rate Structures: The Case of Electricity,"* in Charles J. Cicchetti and John J. Jurewitz, *Studies in Electric Utility Regulation* (Cambridge, Mass.: Ballinger Publishing Co., 1975); Kahn, *Eco-*

nomics of Regulation, pp. 87-109.

[34] Charles J. Cicchetti, "The Design of Electricity Tariffs," *Public Utility Fortnightly,* August 25, 1975, p. 25.

[35] Floyd B. Adams, "Calculating Impact of Lifeline Rates," *Public Power,* March-April 1976, p. 13.

[36] State of New York, Public Service Commission, Statement of Policy on Advertising and Promotional Practices of Public Utilities, February 25, 1977. Order Denying Petitions for Rehearing, July 14, 1977.

[37] Order No. 517, Fuel Adjustment Clauses in Wholesale Rate Schedules, 52 FPC 1304 (1974).

[38] These clauses are seen as consistent with other purposes of the House bill since they are a general method of flattening rates, since increases are applied to each kilowatt-hour. Brancato, "New Approaches," p. 46.

[39] Section 501(1).

[40] Executive Office of the President, Energy Policy and Planning, *The National Energy Plan,* April 29, 1977, pp. 87-88.

[41] Gainesville Utilities Dept. v. Florida Power Corp.

[42] Otter Tail Power Co. v. United States, 410 U.S. 366.

[43] Ibid., p. 374.

[44] U.S. Congress, House, Subcommittee on Energy and Power, House Committee on Interstate and Foreign Commerce, *Hearings on H.R. 6831, the National Energy Act, Title I, Part E, Public Utilities, and H.R. 6660, Electric Utilities Act of 1977,* May 20, 1977, Statement of George Spiegel, Spiegel & McDiarmid (hereinafter referred to as *Hearings*).

[45] Otter Tail Power Co. v. United States, 410 U.S. p. 380.

[46] Under existing law, suspension of rate increases and the length thereof is discretionary. Municipal Light Boards of Reading and Wakefield v. FPC, 450 F.2d 1341 (1971).

[47] The Federal Power Commission has jurisdiction to consider differences between wholesale and retail rates under the Federal Power Act under the provisions prohibiting undue discrimination. FPC v. Conway Corp., 426 U.S. 271 (1976).

[48] Alex Radin, "Outlook and Insights, Improving FPC Regulation," *Public Power,* May-June 1976, pp. 8-9; Statement of G. Stanley Hill, director of Power Supply and Planning, Oglethorpe Electric Membership Corporation in *Hearings*.

[49] FPC v. Conway Corp., 426 U.S. 271 (1976).

[50] Cities of Mishawaka, Indiana v. Indiana & Michigan Electric Co., No. 76-2226 (7th Cir. August 16, 1977), slip op at 8.

[51] Ibid.

[52] For example, Carolina Power & Light Co., Docket No. E-8884, 52 FPC 399, 991 (1974).

[53] See generally, Louis Flax and Mark Drazen, *Current Proposals for Changes in the Design of Electric Utility Rates* (Washington, D.C.: National Association of Manufacturers, 1976); Edison Electric Institute, *Analysis of the Provisions of H.R. 8444 that Affect Electric Utilities,* August 1977 (hereafter referred to as *EEI Analysis*).

[54] *EEI Analysis,* introduction, p. iii; Statement of Sherwood Smith, president, Carolina Power & Light Co., in *Hearings,* pp. 3, 6.

[55] Sherwood Smith, Statement in *Hearings,* p. 8; Haskell Wald, "Recent Proposals for Redesigning Electric Utility Rates," *Public Utility Fortnightly,* September 13, 1973, p. 27. The NARUC Executive Committee, in urging Congress to transform the utility ratemaking provisions of the act into recommendations, stated that rates based strictly on costs could be interpreted as requiring higher residential and lower industrial rates. NARUC Bulletin No. 34-1977, August 22, 1977, p. 22.

[56] Flax and Drazen, *Current Proposals,* pp. 34-46.

[57] Grainger, "A Practical Approach to Peak Day Pricing," p. 20.

[58] Robert M. Granger, "On the Allocation of Capacity Costs," *Public Utilities Fortnightly,* December 16, 1976, p. 26.

[59] *EEI Analysis,* p. 15.

[60] Flax and Drazen, *Current Proposals,* p. 46.

[61] Grainger, "A Practical Approach to Peak Day Pricing," p. 21.

[62] John T. Wenders, "The Misapplication of the Theory of Peak Load Pricing to the Electric Utility Industry," *Public Utility Fortnightly,* December 4, 1975, p. 22.

[63] Colorado Interstate Gas Co. v. FPC, 324 U.S. 581 (1945); Atlantic Seaboard Corp., 11 FPC 43 (1952). Recently the commission has assigned 75 percent of fixed capacity costs to be allocated on the basis of annual sales, with only 25 percent of such costs to be allocated on the basis of system peak usage. Consolidated Gas Supply Corp. v. FPC, 520 F.2d 1176 (D.C. Cir. 1975).

[64] *Wall Street Journal,* August 12, 1977, p. 1.

[65] *EEI Analysis,* p. 14.

[66] The Illinois Commerce Commission has recently held that a lifeline rate violated the antidiscrimination provision of its Public Utilities Act. American Bar Association Annual Report, Section of Public Utility Law, 1977, p. 119.

[67] Bluefield Water Works & Improvement Co. v. Public Service Commission, 262 U.S. 679 (1923).

[68] Joe D. Pace, "Lifeline Rates: Will They Do the Job?" *Public Power,* November-December 1975, p. 21.

[69] Under both House and Senate bills, natural gas prices for high priority (that is, residential and small commercial use) uses are to be based on the system average cost of gas for the twelve months ending with passage of the bill. Other costs and increases in the cost of gas above this level will be paid by other customers.

[70] Kahn, *Economics of Regulation,* p. 68; Pace, "Lifeline Rates"; Jules Joskow, "What Comes Next in Retail Electric Rate Policies," *Public Power,* July-August 1975, p. 17.

[71] State of New York, Public Service Commission, Statement of Policy; "Public Utilities: The Allowance of Advertising Expenditures for Rate-Making Purposes—Is This Trip Really Necessary?" *Oklahoma Law Review,* vol. 29 (1976), p. 202.

[72] *EEI Analysis,* p. 19.

[73] Ibid., pp. 22-23.

[74] Notice of Proposed Rulemaking, Docket No. RM77-2, August 15, 1977. The Chairman of the Federal Trade Commission and the Acting Assistant Attorney General, Antitrust Division, Department of Justice, supported the limited disclosure of these data.

[75] *EEI Analysis,* pp. 38-39.

[76] Testimony of William A. Duncan, president, Kentucky Utilities Company, in *Hearings.*

[77] *EEI Analysis,* p. 48.

[78] Under existing law, the Federal Power Commission cannot award attorney's fees to intervenors in cases before it. Greene County Planning Board v. FPC, Nos. 76-4151 and 76-4153 (2d Cir. June 30, 1977).

[79] *EEI Analysis,* pp. 33, 51.

[80] Ibid., p. 40.

[81] Ibid., p. 44.